MW01045940

CELEBRATING

FRIENDSHIP

ANNE WILSON

Glendale Heights, IL 60139

Compiled by Anne Wilson

Cover Design by Design Dynamics
Illustrations by Joanne Fink

Published by Great Quotations, Inc.

Library of Congress Catalog Card Number : 98-075791

ISBN: 1-56245-361-0

Printed in Hong Kong

This collection of quotations on love and friendship

will bring a smile and warm the heart of all

who share in the true meaning of these words.

"A friend is someone who understands your past, believes in your future, and accepts you today just the way you are."

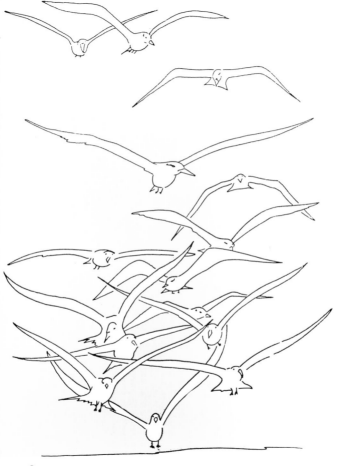

"Friendship is what makes you think almost as much for someone else as you do for yourself."

"We cannot tell the precise moment
when friendship is formed. As in
filling a vessel drop by drop, there is
at last a drop that makes it run over;
so in a series of kindnesses, there is
a last one that makes the heart run
over."

Samuel Johnson

"Let us be first to give a friendly sign, to nod first, smile first, speak first and if such a thing is necessary— forgive first."

"Love is a butterfly, which
when pursued is just beyond
your grasp, but if you will
sit down quietly it may
alight upon you."

Nathaniel Hawthorne

"The only way to have a friend is to be one."

Ralph Waldo Emerson

"Life is to be fortified by many friendships—to love and to be loved is the greatest happiness of existence."

Sydney Smith

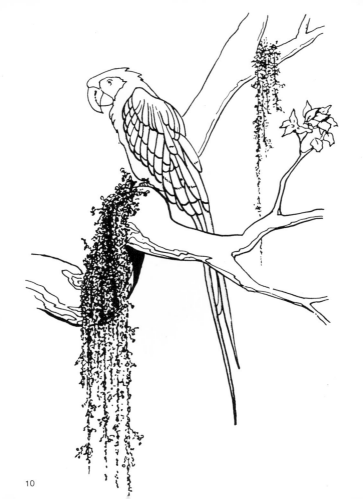

"You can always tell a real friend; when you've made a fool of yourself, he doesn't feel you've done a permanent job."

Laurence J. Peter

"A friend is one who knows all about you and still likes you."

"Wherever you are it is
your own friends who
make your world."

William James

14

"Of all the music that reaches farthest into heaven, it is the beating of a loving heart."

Henry Ward Beecher

"A friend is a person with whom you dare to be yourself."

*"Friendship improves
happiness and abates
misery by doubling our joy
and dividing our grief."*

Addison

"A friend will joyfully sing with you when you are on the mountain top, and silently walk beside you through the valley."

"When a friend asks,
there is no
tomorrow."

"We pardon to the extent that we love."

Francois, Duc De La Rochefoucauld

"The best antique
is an old friend."

"Let no one who loves be called unhappy. Even love unreturned has its rainbow."

James Matthew Barrie

"There are those who pass like ships in the night.
Who meet for a moment, then sail out of sight
with never a backwards glance of regret;
folks we know briefly then quickly forget.
Then there are friends who sail together
through quiet waters and stormy weather
helping each other through joy and through strife.
And they are the kind who give meaning to life."

"*The world is so empty if one thinks only of mountains, rivers, and cities; but to know someone here and there who thinks and feels with us, and who, though distant, is close to us in spirit, this makes the earth an inhabited garden.*"

Goethe

"A real friend warms you by his presence, trusts you with his secrets, and remembers you in his prayers."

"A successful marriage requires falling in love many times— with the same person."

"Love is something eternal— the aspect may change, but not the essence."

Vincent Van Gogh

"A friend will strengthen you with his prayers, bless you with his love, and encourage you with his hope."

"We are all born for love.

...It is the principle
of existence."

Disraeli-Sybil

"Until I truly loved, I was alone."

Caroline Sheridan Nordon

"Blessed are they who have the gift of making friends, for it is one of God's best gifts. It involves many things, but above all, the power of going out of one's self, and appreciating whatever is noble and loving in another."

Thomas Hughes

"Love is the triumph of imagination over intelligence."

H. L. Mencken

"False friendship, like the ivy, decays and ruins the walls it embraces, but true friendship gives new life and animation to the object it supports."

Burton

"In the last analysis, love is only the reflection of a person's own worthiness from other people."

Ralph Waldo Emerson

"A true friend is forever a friend."

"*True friends don't sympathize with your weakness—they help summon your strength.*"

*"The heart is a brittle thing,
and one false vow can
break it."*

E.G. Bulver-Lytton

"*Friendship is a living thing that lasts only as long as it is nourished with kindness, sympathy, and understanding.*"

"Some people have their first dollar. The person who is really rich is the one who still has his first friend."

"One word frees us of all the weight and pain of life: that word is love."

Sophocles

"The great acts of love
are done by those
who are habitually
performing small acts
of kindness."

"You are the
sunshine of
my life."

Stevie Wonder

"The bank of friendship cannot exist for long without deposits."

"A true friend thinks of you when all others are thinking of themselves."

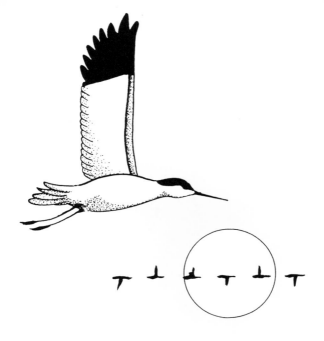

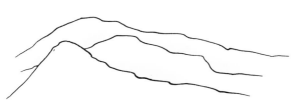

"Love is knowing that even when you are alone, you will never be lonely again."

"Friendship is unnecessary, like philosophy, like art... it has no survival value: rather it is one of those things that give value to survival."

C.S. Lewis

"The supreme happiness of life is the conviction that we are loved."

Victor Hugo

"Life is to be fortified by many friendships. To love and to be loved is the greatest happiness in existence."

Sydney Smith

"Genuine friendship is like good health; its value is seldom known until it is lost."

"Oh, the comfort, the inexpressible comfort, of feeling safe with a person, having neither to weigh thought nor measure words, but pouring them all right out, just as they are, chaff and grain together; certain that a faithful hand will take and sift them, keep what is worth keeping and with a breath of kindness blow the rest away."

"The greatest service one can perform is to be a friend to someone. Friendship is not only doing something for someone, but it is caring for someone, which is what every person needs."

C. Neil Strait

"A friend is one who walks in when the rest of the world walks out."

"Be gentle with me, new love. Treat me tenderly. I need the gentle touch, the soft voice, the candlelight after nine."

Rod McKuen

"Friendship is the only cement that will hold the world together."

"Time is
Too slow for those who Wait,
Too swift for those who Fear,
Too long for those who Grieve,
Too short for those who Rejoice;
But for those who Love,
Time is Eternity."

"Love is that condition in which the happiness of another person is essential to your own joy."

Robert A. Heinlin

"Love is the gentle smile upon the lips of beauty."

Kahil Gibran

"In love there are
two things;
bodies and
words."

Joyce Carol Oates

"Love is the poetry of the senses."

Honore de Balzac

"Love doesn't make the world go 'round, but it makes the ride worthwhile."

"There is no disguise
which can for long
conceal love."

Francois, Duc De La Rochefoucauld

"You can give without loving, but you can never love without giving."

"Never forget that the most powerful force on earth is love."

Nelson Rockefeller

"In real love you want the other person's good.

In romantic love you want the other person."

Margaret Anderson

"The way to love anything is to realize it might be lost."

G. K. Chesterton

"Friendship is unneccessary, like philosophy, like art...it has no survival value: rather it is one of those things that give value to survival."

C.S. Lewis

"Love doesn't make the world go 'round, but it makes the ride worthwhile."

Other Titles by Great Quotations, Inc.

Hard Covers

Ancient Echoes
Behold the Golfer
Commanders in Chief
The Essence of Music
First Ladies
Good Lies for Ladies
Great Quotes From Great Teachers
Great Women
I Thought of You Today
Journey to Success
Just Between Friends
Lasting Impressions
My Husband My Love
Never Ever Give Up
The Passion of Chocolate
Peace Be With You
The Perfect Brew
The Power of Inspiration
Sharing the Season
Teddy Bears
There's No Place Like Home

Paperbacks

301 Ways to Stay Young
ABC's of Parenting
Angel-grams
African American Wisdom
Astrology for Cats
Astrology for Dogs
The Be-Attitudes
Birthday Astrologer
Can We Talk
Chocoholic Reasonettes
Cornerstones of Success
Daddy & Me
Erasing My Sanity
Graduation is Just the Beginning
Grandma I Love You
Happiness is Found Along the Way
Hooked on Golf
Ignorance is Bliss
In Celebration of Women
Inspirations
Interior Design for Idiots

Great Quotations, Inc.
1967 Quincy Court
Glendale Heights,IL 60139 USA
Phone: 630-582-2800   Fax: 630-582-2813
http://www.greatquotations.com

Other Titles by Great Quotations, Inc.

Paperbacks

I'm Not Over the Hill
Life's Lessons
Looking for Mr. Right
Midwest Wisdom
Mommy & Me
Mother, I Love You
The Mother Load
Motivating Quotes
Mrs.Murphy's Laws
Mrs. Webster's Dictionary
Only A Sister
The Other Species
Parenting 101
Pink Power
Romantic Rhapsody
The Secret Langauge of Men
The Secret Langauge of Women
The Secrets in Your Name
A Servant's Heart
Social Disgraces
Stress or Sanity
A Teacher is Better Than
Teenage of Insanity
Touch of Friendship
Wedding Wonders
Words From the Coach

Perpetual Calendars

365 Reasons to Eat Chocolate
Always Remember Who Loves You
Best Friends
Coffee Breaks
The Dog Ate My Car Keys
Extraordinary Women
Foundations of Leadership
Generations
The Heart That Loves
The Honey Jar
I Think My Teacher Sleeps at School
I'm a Little Stressed
Keys to Success
Kid Stuff
Never Never Give Up
Older Than Dirt
Secrets of a Successful Mom
Shopoholic
Sweet Dreams
Teacher Zone
Tee Times
A Touch of Kindness
Apple a Day
Golf Forever
Quotes From Great Women
Teacher Are First Class